Texas Tomorrow

Texas Tomorrow

An Economic Plan for Texas in the
21st Century

Raul Torres, CPA

authorHOUSE®

AuthorHouse™ LLC
1663 Liberty Drive
Bloomington, IN 47403
www.authorhouse.com
Phone: 1-800-839-8640

Published by AuthorHouse   08/06/2013

ISBN: 978-1-4918-0519-0 (sc)
ISBN: 978-1-4918-0520-6 (e)

Library of Congress Control Number: 2013914296

Contents

Introduction..1

Prioritize..4

   Recommendations..6

Stabilize...8

   Recommendations..12

Incentivize...13

   Economic Development...14

   Provide For A Highly Skilled And Educated Workforce..........15

      It Starts With Secondary Education Reform.......................16

      Standardized High Stakes Testing.......................................17

      School Finance..20

   Recommendations..24

Supplement To Texas Tomorrow..27

Texas Should Move to Priority Based Budgeting.............................29

   Background...29

   Understanding the Texas budget process....................................29

   Priority Based Budgeting...30

   Anatomy of a Priority Based Budget..31

   Advantages...31

   Setting Priorities...32

   Where to Look...32

      Citizen Input...33

      Other States..33

   Recommendations..33

The Texas Budget Process Should Be Modified..............................35

   Summary..35

   Background...35

Budget Principles 36
Better questions to ask 36
Texas Budget Process...37
Next Steps 37
Measuring performance 38
Recommendations..38
It's Time for Cost-benefit Analysis of State Spending.................40
Summary...40
Background..40
Recommendations..41
Rethinking Regulation in Texas 43
Summary...43
Background..43
Recommendations..44
Texas Agencies Should Improve Back Office Efficiency.............47
Summary...47
Background..47
Recommendations..48
The State Should Utilize Statewide Building Maintenance Services
Contracts 49
Summary...49
Background..49
Recommendations..50
Texas Should Rethink Its Economic Development Strategy..........51
Summary...51
Background..51
Recommendations..52
Reforming Public Education in Texas.....................................54
Summary...54
Background..54
System ownership 55
Chipping away at change 56
Addressing the substantial drop out rate in Texas schools.......56
Recommendations..57

It's Time to Rethink Standardized Testing..................................59
    Summary 59
    Background 59
    Enter Standardized Testing.......................................60
    How Much Does It Cost...61
    Is It Working...62
    There are Alternatives 64
    Recommendations...64
It's Time to Rethink How To Fund Public Education....................66
    Summary 66
    Background 66
    Effects of Recent Cuts...67
    Current system 67
    Deficiencies 68
    Identifying the costs of educating a student..............68
    Recommendations...69
Use Technology to Reduce the Cost of Higher Education............71
    Summary 71
    Background 71
    Recommendations...72

About the Author...75
Endnotes...77

This book is dedicated to all of the men and women whose abiding faith in a Creator, love freedom and whose entrepreneurial spirit is largely responsible for building America into the world's most productive, creative, and prosperous nation the world has ever seen.

And to Ronald Reagan, whose wit, charm, and leadership gave us hope to believe in ourselves once again.

"I've spoken of the shining city all my political life, but I don't know if I ever quite communicated what I saw when I said it. But in my mind it was a tall proud city built on rocks stronger than oceans, wind-swept, God-blessed, and teeming with people of all kinds living in harmony and peace, a city with free ports that hummed with commerce and creativity, and if there had to be city walls, the walls had doors and the doors were open to anyone with the will and the heart to get here."

RONALD REAGAN, farewell address, Jan. 11, 1989

Introduction

Imagine a place where jobs are plentiful, people are free to worship as they please, where people are personally responsible for their actions, neighbors help out neighbors in need, where a good education is the standard rather than the exception, where the American Dream is celebrated regularly, and where government is limited. That is my vision and hope for the State of Texas in the 21st century.

It is no secret to the rest of the nation that the State of Texas has something unique to offer. Despite a national recession that has crippled the economy, our state economy has continued to grow. Texas is consistently among the top states in the nation for job creation, economic growth, and business climate. Individuals and businesses are attracted to moving here because of our low level of taxation, predictable and low levels of regulation, strong property rights protection, sound justice system, and minimal dependence on the federal government. Texas is a great place to live, but it can be better.

During the 2011 Legislative Session, Texas faced an unprecedented budget shortfall, a hole that was caused by overspending and the routine practice of forcing future legislatures to pay the costs. In 2011, those who voted for the appropriations bill deferred Medicaid spending, cut funding to education, did not fund k-12 enrollment growth, and did not use funds for their purpose in certifying the budget.

Raising revenue is not the answer. We cannot tax our way to prosperity, and I believe there are better ways to solve these challenges. Some ideas are new, many are not, but I believe we must have a plan to foster continuous improvement.

"Texas Tomorrow: An Economic Plan for Texas in the 21st Century," presents a blueprint for growing the Texas economy resulting in a higher quality of life for its citizens. It promotes innovative and creative ideas to prioritize state spending, stabilizing the state's taxing and regulatory programs, incentivizing the job creators and calls for true public school reform. The blueprint also shows us that there are alternatives to higher taxes and deeper spending cuts that rob our citizens of their ability to live, work and prosper. And finally it calls for the legislature to take bold steps to rein in spending, encourage economic development and for it to take a real leadership role as Texas transforms itself into a 21st century state."

In March of 2012, I released a version of my plan for comment and recommendations from citizens, policy makers and business and trade groups. I want to thank all of you who offered comments and made this a better document. During the past five years I have spent most of my time campaigning or serving as a member of the

Texas House of Representatives. It was during this time that I had the privilege to meet people from all over Texas. We often spoke of our many concerns, hopes and dreams. These conversations inspired me to write this book.

Prioritize

Just like the citizens it governs, government must learn to live within its means. While Texas is a balanced budget state, it does not live within its means. State and local governments have a bad habit of using debt to build and added to that is the question of unfunded pensions. This has resulted in a total debt burden of $286 billion, or $11,117 for each Texan.

Additionally the state used unspent dollars to certify the last budget, and is expected to use $4.9 billion of unspent tax dollars to certify the next budget. Call it what you will, voodoo economics or smoke and mirrors, the budget process in Texas is in itself part of the problem.

Knowing further cuts will be difficult in a state that ranks 50th in per capita spending and that must recover from several program cuts imposed during the last session, Texas must be more efficient and accountable when using citizens' tax dollars.

First and foremost the best way to reduce spending is to prioritize what money is spent. As governments at all levels struggle to meet basic needs with even more limited resources, policy makers seek new ways to balance budgets without raising taxes. Economists agree that higher taxes do not spur economic growth and they understand that stalled economic growth limits revenue available to policy makers. Deciding

For instance, consider the question, "Is that program effective?" This is a fundamentally different question than, "Is that program worthwhile?" Additionally, rather than ask what should be cut, policy makers should ask, "On what do we want to spend the taxpayer's dollars?"

Texas Legislative Budget Board document, "15 Lessons Learned."

how to allocate these resources, or what the state wants to "buy," has become more important than ever.

Taxpayers are demanding to know not only how their money is being spent but how policy makers are making those decisions. Those questions have led to a call for greater transparency of government spending as well as a call for greater transparency of the decision making process that precedes spending decisions.

Priority Based Budgeting (PBB) is a method of setting priorities that provides transparency, accountability, and a method of top down funding that families use every day.

Another key to prioritizing spending is the budget process itself. For the third budget cycle in a row, state leaders have begun the process by ordering across the board cuts or holding spending to past biennium levels that had suffered from across the board cuts. Across the board cuts are not the answer. While they may seem equitable and avoid conflict, they are not strategic and do nothing to shape and reduce the size government; nor, do they create value for taxpayers. In some ways they represent an abdication of the legislature's responsibility to appropriate state revenues. There are better questions for policy makers to ask. But the current system does not provide the necessary guidance or information.

Up until the mid-1970's the Texas budget was based on object of expense which told policy makers what the money was spent on but not where it was spent. In the mid 70's the state moved to program budgeting which told policy makers where tax dollars were being spent but not how they were spent. Then in 1991 Texas moved to performance based budgeting which told policy makers how the money was being spent and tied agency performance to the budget. In that year agencies were required to develop strategic plans so policy makers could gauge the performance of state agencies. While the current system is not perfect, it does position

Texas to move to the next stage of its budget evolution. However, to get there some things need to change.

Measuring agency performance as the means to prepare the Texas budget does not present policy makers with the information they need to assess the value of a program when weighed against its costs.

There is an answer: a cost-benefit analysis can be used to evaluate the desirability of a given program. It will help answer the question of whether a program is worthwhile. This system helps policy makers rank programs according to their effectiveness at achieving desired results. This will ensure that vital services are being funded before less critical ones. And when funding programs, policy makers can begin with programs and efforts with the highest priority and value appropriating dollars efficiently to best serve taxpayers.

Until Texas policy makers set the priorities of government, straighten out the budget process, and receive useful information Texas will remain a debt ridden state burdening its children and threatening its future.

Recommendations

- Texas should implement priority based budgeting;
- Incorporate zero based budgeting into the budget process;
- The Texas Legislature should direct the Legislative Budget Board to design a program that provides a cost-benefit analysis of relevant spending programs. The Texas Legislature should form a statewide citizen-legislature commission to identify and prioritize the core functions of government;

- The Texas Legislative Budget Board in concert with the Texas Department of Information Resources should develop a web based interactive website to seek input into what citizens feel the priorities of government should be;
- Texas should reexamine its budget process to ensure that it provides policy makers and budget writers with the information necessary for them to make informed decisions regarding program funding; and,
- State agencies should be required to include information about how they plan to evaluate the effectiveness of their programs and link their disbursements to evidence.

Stabilize

Stabilize is defined as the quality, state, or degree of being firmly established, not changing or fluctuating, steady in purpose and not subject to insecurity. That is what a good government should offer. While change is necessary, a destabilized environment does not provide the security its citizens or businesses desire in order to make important day-to-day decisions.

For Texas to continue to be a magnet for economic growth it must provide that stable environment. It must provide a stable tax system that is both adequate and fair. It must provide a stable regulatory system that encourages investment while protecting its citizens. And it must stabilize its spending in order to ensure taxpayers keep more of their hard earned money.

Texas has one of the lowest tax burdens in the nation and that is a reason why businesses locate here. But its heavy reliance on property tax unfairly burdens citizens and businesses alike. It also causes problems with the funding of our schools as evidenced by the numerous school funding lawsuits filed over the years. It is also likely that the recently enacted Margin's Tax will need to be changed during the upcoming legislative session. Added to that is a sales tax rate that can be adjusted at the whim of state or local governments. Changes in any of these taxes cost businesses money and do not provide the stability necessary for economic growth.

Texas has and still does rely heavily on oil and gas production taxes. But Texas' economy is shifting to a more service oriented structure and the current tax system is not reflective of that. One suggestion is to lower and broaden the Margin's Tax to cover more businesses and business types. Every business should pay their fair share for the basic services Texas government provides. But that price should not be so steep that business owners, and eventually consumers, can't afford it. Another option being discussed is to eliminate property taxes in favor of an increased sales tax. Whatever the decision is it should take a super majority of the legislature to make further changes to the amount and type of tax levied. That being said I believe we can eliminate the Margin's Tax and over a period of 10 years transition period eliminate the property tax in lieu of a broader expanded sales tax. I project this transformation would create an economic boom for the state that would lead the nation for many years.

Another area of concern for businesses small and large is the regulatory environment. Regulations always come with a cost of compliance, permitting, and/or licensing. While business owners must pay the cost, ultimately the consumer picks up the tab. But consumers get hit twice by the cost of regulation. They, as tax payers, also pay the cost that government incurs to enforce the regulation and issue the permits and licenses. For these reasons burdensome regulations are a hindrance to economic growth.

There is no doubt that government regulation is needed, but there remains a question of how much is truly necessary. There is also question as to how those regulations are carried out, especially the permitting that they require. Identifying the many regulations that businesses operate under and taxpayers pay for is like peeling an onion. One finds layer after layer of them. Identifying the true cost of those regulations is no less difficult. There is much that can be done to lessen the regulatory burden on businesses and to lessen the costs to taxpayers and consumers.

While many of the regulations Texas businesses must face are federal, the state can reduce the burden to those businesses by being smarter about how it regulates. For instance a dry cleaner is required to pay a yearly $2,000 fee to the Texas Commission on Environmental Quality in case of ground contamination due to a chemical spill. That dry cleaner could purchase a $1,000 insurance policy that would provide much more coverage than $2,000 if remediation is needed. Another example of the problem is getting permits needed to construct an industrial plant. Many projects require local, state, and federal permits. The most onerous are required by the Clean Air Act, and some require multiple state and federal permits. The cost to business is not only in the consultants and staff time devoted to navigating these regulations, but in the delay of construction.

State spending is the key to keeping tax rates and business costs low and stabilizing that spending will take innovative and new ways of doing business. For example, in 2010 the State of Texas spent over $40 million for building and maintenance expenses. These expenses included repair for elevators, windows, doors, overhead doors, painting and carpentry. The process for securing such work is repeated by each agency for each maintenance item needed. This is a costly and cumbersome process. It is estimated that securing a contract can cost up to $2,000 and issuing purchase orders under that contract can cost hundreds of dollars. The current system also lacks economies of scale. Why isn't this handled as one service for all state agencies to ensure the lowest possible price for services at the lowest possible cost to government?

And finally, Texas must improve its back office efficiency while achieving a high level of customer satisfaction. Governments at all levels are constantly working to become more efficient in an effort to save tax dollars and better serve its citizens. It is not uncommon for state agencies to identify private sector best practices that would achieve these goals.

For a number of years industrial sector businesses have employed a method of improving quality and reducing the costs of services called Lean Six Sigma. While developed for manufacturing processes, its principles can be applied to many business processes that deliver a product to a customer. In 2011, I helped author and pass S.B. 563 which directed the Texas Workforce Commission, "to establish a pilot program to improve the efficiency and quality of operations while reducing costs, and to adopt a structured approach for identifying the wasteful use of state resources and improving processes."

After the pilot project concluded, it was found to be a complete success. The program on which it was used saw an increase in productivity and services provided while reducing waiting times and cost. In this test of Lean Six Sigma's methodology at the Texas Workforce Commission, all of this resulted in more people put to work more quickly in Texas.

As can be seen from the above discussion providing a stable base for job growth can come from many directions and my recommendations are only a start. I think, we can all agree that steps to stabilize Texas must be taken soon and built upon from there. In that way Texas can continue to be a bright beacon in a nation enveloped in the darkness of a failed economy.

Recommendations

- A state task force should be established to identify, for purposes of elimination, all regulations and permits and study their effectiveness, usefulness, and impacts on the economy and government spending with a focus on those that are 10 years old and older;

- The Legislature should direct the Office of State-Federal Relations to engage the Texas congressional delegation to encourage federal regulatory agencies to work with Texas regulatory agencies to align regulatory and permitting requirements;
- The legislature should expand the concept of the Coastal Coordination Council to all permits required of businesses operating in Texas;
- The legislature should require a cost-benefit analysis of any regulation or permit required by statute or administrative rule before that statute or rule is adopted;
- The Council on Competitive Government (CCG) should declare the maintenance of facilities as a statewide service and issue a contract for such service;
- The Texas Facilities Commission (TFC) should develop a web based automated system to be used by state agencies when maintenance is needed; and,
- Texas agencies, boards, and commissions should employ the Integrated Theory of Constraints Lean Six Sigma methodology to improve back office operations.

Incentivize

 Businesses rarely make a decision to locate their investment based solely on financial incentives. A group of Cornell researchers found that factors such as skilled labor, a strong infrastructure and good schools offer more incentive for businesses to start up or relocate. They also found that, "Tax abatement subsidies to individual firms do not significantly impact firm decisions to relocate or expand."[3] To maintain the momentum we've already built Texas must provide an improved business climate through a mix of pro-growth policies and financial incentives. Most importantly it must provide a highly skilled and educated workforce.

As mentioned earlier, financial incentives are not the only incentive businesses look for, but it is one of a number of things that will attract new businesses. There are those that believe that government should not use public funds to subsidize private enterprise. The Texas Public Policy Foundation takes the position that the best way for government to attract new business is to get out of the way and let the private sector operate in reaction to the incentives provided through the free market system. There is also truth to the belief that in many cases the economic benefit a business brings never offset the cost of the new infrastructure the public sector must provide. Nevertheless, offering financial incentives is required to maintain a competitive position in today's competitive economy.

Economic Development

Most economic development is done at the local level, but the state is heavily invested in economic development. One of its eight statewide goals is promoting economic development and in fiscal 2010 it spent $9.3 billion doing just that.[4] It did so through a number of agencies as well as through the Department of Economic Development and Tourism within the office of the Governor which oversees more than 67 different programs.

In 2011 the Texas Legislature formed the Select Committee on Economic Development to review state economic development programs and make recommendations to the Legislature, including whether or not to consolidate the programs or have one agency in charge of economic development.

At a recent meeting of the Select Committee on Economic Development, one of the committee's subcommittee chairmen was reported to have said that, "he has heard criticism that the Texas diversified approach can be confusing or slows down the recruitment process."[5]

The Texas Department of Economic Development was formed in 1997 as an outgrowth of the Texas Department of Commerce. The new agency was tasked with the Texas Smart Jobs Program and tourism as well as economic development duties. It suffered through a number of mismanagement issues and in 2003 it was restructured and moved to the office of the Governor. It was thought that it would be more effective there as it coordinated economic development activities across the many state agencies that played a key role in the state's economic development. Others thought the move would give the Governor too much authority over economic development for Texas.

Since that move the state's economic development process has been mired in and threatened by politics. It may be time to reestablish the agency as well as the commission that oversaw it.

In testimony given to the Select Committee on Economic Development witnesses told the committee that other challenges to economic development in Texas exist in education, transportation, water, health care and increasing competition from other states.

Provide For A Highly Skilled And Educated Workforce

Texas businesses need highly skilled and educated employees. And there is plenty of evidence that the Texas system of education is not providing them. The debate over public education has devolved into a blame game of accountability rather than a discussion of why students are not performing and are dropping out of school. The statistics are frightening. Texas ranks 49th in performance on the verbal SAT and 46th in math and 43rd in the percent of students graduating from high school. And the number of students dropping out of high school and college is staggering. It is estimated that by 2020, 60% of all jobs will require a college degree. Many of the remaining will require some sort of technical or trade certifications. The problem is that only 39% of adult Texans are expected to have a post-secondary education degree.

Things must change if we are to meet that 2020 challenge and businesses and industry are paying close attention. They frequently point to their need for a workforce with the basic skills to help them succeed in a competitive marketplace.

It Starts With Secondary Education Reform

While the Texas Constitution guarantees an "efficient system of public free schools,"[6] it has been acknowledged that efficiency has two components: finance and quality. Traditionally, quality has been viewed as tied to the amount of money spent on it, but in reality quality and money are mutually exclusive. One does not, and should not, depend upon the other.

Over the years the courts have had one consistent message to policy makers—efficiency goes beyond money. While the courts have been asked to rule on the equitableness of the finance system each has taken the opportunity to point out that money is not the only issue or the only solution.

Recent years have seen many changes in the delivery system of education in Texas. The allowance of charter schools, home rule school districts, and home schooling has changed the educational system landscape in Texas. But more can and must be done if Texas wants to achieve the vision of those who drafted and adopted the 1876 constitution. Better utilization of these non-traditional forms of public education will likely benefit students, taxpayers, and eventually the Texas economy.

One of the elements lacking in the public school system is an effective way of dealing with the high rate of dropouts in secondary education. There has also been a drive toward preparing students for college rather than preparing them for careers. While programs have developed to address both, it has been localized to specific school districts or even selected campuses. Texas has worked to address the issue of students dropping out of high school but more can be done. Students drop out of school for many reasons and there is no one solution to the problem. But the system itself contributes to the problem. Our schools are geared toward readying students for four-year degree programs. While every student should have some post-secondary education, not every student wants to or should go to college. For example there is a shortage of skilled tradesmen and women. What good is it to teach a student how to design a car if there is no one skilled enough to build or repair it?

Providing career based curriculums to students is on¹e way to keep students in school. The student who wants to be a welder does not need the same math education as one who wants to be an economist. The economist doesn't need the same math that a theoretical physicist would need. But these curriculums will not be successful if students do not know what they want or have the ability to do. Career counseling and aptitude testing has taken a back seat as schools have had to tighten their financial belts and prepare their students to take the standardized tests that have become so popular with policy makers. Helping our children realize their potential and decide what they are capable of and want to do in life should be one of the top goals in secondary education.

Standardized High Stakes Testing

Another area of concern is standardized high stakes testing. Students who do not perform well on these tests are likely to drop out thinking there is no hope of graduating. Even some legislative leaders think the stakes are too high and put too much pressure on students and teachers. That pressure has affected not only student performance, but how education is delivered. Many think that testing has gotten out of hand due to the number of tests students must now take. Many others believe that it forces teachers to teach to the test rather than educate our workforce of tomorrow. Some believe that testing is not a good gauge of student learning and is not a good way of assessing the effectiveness of our schools in teaching students because they are flawed in their design. Added to all of that, there is a strong belief among policy makers and taxpayers that standardized testing has cost too much without providing the expected results.

As far back as the mid 1990's policy makers were aware that the remediation problem existed and was getting worse. The Texas Comptroller of Public Accounts recommended holding public secondary schools accountable for the basic skills of their graduates entering college. In that policy recommendation it was noted that "students in secondary schools have been required to take examinations testing basic skills as a graduation requirement since 1985."[7] Because of Texas' student performance when measured against other states and nations and the increasing cost of public education, taxpayers urged lawmakers to develop a system that would evaluate whether they were getting their money's worth. So policy makers rushed into standardized testing. The first, The Texas Assessment of Basic Skills, test was administered in the 1979-1980 school year. And now, more than thirty years later the state is still wrestling with the same problem.

The drive for accountability has been augmented by a multi-billion dollar industry hungry for public education dollars. The state contracted with NCS Pearson Inc., the nation's largest testing company, to develop, administer and grade the State's STARR test. That contract is worth $500 million dollars through 2015. By 2015 the state will have paid Pearson nearly $1.2 billion for developing standardized tests and related materials since

2000.[8] In 2012 the cost is $90 million and expected to be near $100 million in 2015.

But that is not the only cost of these tests. In 2004 the state signed a $17.7 million four year deal with Grow network for study guides designed for high school students that didn't pass the TAKS test. And the state also purchased summer remediation study guides from Pearson at the cost of $8.8 million for the period from 2006 through 2011.[9]

Districts across the state have reported spending millions in local district funds to administer the tests. Because of the number of tests some schools have had to hire test administrators. They've had to hire additional part time teachers or teacher aides to monitor hallways and bathrooms. And administrators must spend time reading, "a 156-page manual, plus a 47-page security supplement, to prepare for a testing season that runs from October through July."[10]

With the amount of tax dollars spent on testing, it's interesting to note that on the recently administered STAAR tests, students scored better in math, biology, and geography than they did in reading comprehension. One has to ask the question, "If they can't read how can they can pass anything else?" As it turns out the test design may be flawed. A recent study released by University of Texas at Austin professor Walter Stroup came to the conclusion that because of the design of the tests, "they are virtually useless at measuring the effects of classroom instruction." [11]

Perhaps it is time to disassociate measuring college readiness and assessing financial accountability. No test of student achievement is a true measure of the effectiveness of our educational system. But there are tools the state can use to assess a student's readiness for college. And other states are using those tools. Both the PSAT and the pre-ACT tests can be effective tools for measuring preparedness in the sophomore and junior years. And since most students don't need full course instructions to be prepared that lost ground can be made up in a year or less.

School Finance

Not long after the 82nd legislative special session adjourned six lawsuits were filed in district court in Austin, Texas asking that the court find the system of public school finance unconstitutional because it is not efficient. The tussle over school funding has gone on since the 1970's. The latest round was spurred by a $5.4 billion dollar reduction in school funding by state policy makers.

The law suits center around three main issues: efficiency, adequacy, and meaningful discretion. Those arguing that the system is not efficient fall into three categories. One group argues that the system is inequitable, another argues that the cap on charter schools and the prohibition of using state funding for charter school facilities is inefficient, and the third argues that since the state doesn't know how much it costs to educate a student there is no way the system could be efficient. The adequacy issue centers on the argument that the state has failed to provide enough funding, didn't fund growth in enrollment, and didn't provide additional funds at a time when it raised accountability standards. Meaningful discretion centers on the argument that the state has imposed a statewide property tax because it limits the amount local districts can tax.

Local property tax revenue currently provides over 55% of the revenue in the system.[12] As long as public school funding is rooted in property taxes inequity will continue. In 2010-2011, according to the Texas Education Agency, the school districts in the top 15% of wealth had over $2 billion left in taxing capacity while districts in the bottom 15% of wealth had $0 left in taxing capacity. According to the Comptroller of Public Accounts in

2008-2009, the state spent $56.6 billion on public education. $20.3 billion (36%) was provided by the state, $31.7 billion (56%) was provided by local sources, and $4.5 billion (8%) came from Federal sources including American Reinvestment and Recovery Act monies.[13]

The current system of public school finance is a convoluted collection of weights and formulas written in a 50 page document to try explain how it works.[14] Many of its weights, rules and regulations haven't been updated in decades. An example is the Cost of Education Index (CEI) which is used to adjust for the geographic variation in known resource costs and costs of education. But that index hasn't been adjusted since 1991. "Research indicates that the state could save billions by aligning the CEI with today's actual cost differentials."[15] Another is the state facilities funding system guarantee that has not changed from the original $35 yield per penny per average daily attendance adopted in 1999 although the cost of construction has doubled since then.[16]

It's time to re-examine how the state uses state funding to help finance public education. The key to accountability may well lay with the local districts themselves. After all the best form of government is that which is closest to the people. Perhaps it is time to free public schools from the many mandates the legislature has imposed over the years and not hold funding hostage. Perhaps it is time for the state to get out of the way and allow parents and taxpayers to hold their local districts accountable.

Continues with higher education

The greatest barrier to higher education has become the cost to students and their parents. The cost of higher education has risen faster than the cost of medical care in the United States and the cost of course materials has risen faster than the rate of inflation. Students are graduating with record debt in the form of student loans and prepaid tuition programs are having a hard time making good on their promises. Not all is doom and gloom; there is a light at the end of the tunnel. And the way is being lit by technology.

Texas institutions of higher education, led by the Texas Higher Education Coordinating Board (THECB), have done well in the utilization of instructional technology. There are hundreds of online courses available to students through individual two year and four year institutions, technical colleges, and virtual networks. More can and should be done. Like most areas, education is stuck in a costly bricks and mortar mindset. Its focus is on face to face instruction with little regard to the savings that the use of technology can bring. According to the THECB, in 2011 alone, institutions were expected to pay over $17 billion in capital costs. Almost half of the capital costs will be for new construction and a third of it for repair and renovation of existing facilities. Less than 1% was expected to be spent on information resources.[17]

Not only is education stuck in the bricks and mortar mindset but it is also stuck in the printed and bound mindset. According to Barbara Chow of the Hewlett Foundation, another study found that 60% of the students who dropped out of college said that the cost of textbooks and other expenses besides tuition had affected them financially.[18] This year students will spend over $1000 for books and supplies. These costs can be minimized by students who purchase used books or rent books when available. They can also recover some of the cost at the end of a semester by selling their books to resellers or other students. More can be saved by the purchase of e-texts although those come with a time limit and cannot be resold.

One avenue being explored by educators is the use of open education resources (OER). These texts can be purchased from online retailers such as Amazon for as little as $5. They can also be purchased as printed volumes or even printed and bound volumes for far less than the $100-$200 cost of traditional textbooks. Other advantages to OER are that information can be tailored to a specific instructor's and/or student's needs and information can be updated immediately. Open course libraries have been developed in other states that have saved students as much as $100 per course. Rice University has developed OER through its Connexions program. The program has used private funding to develop the course material so far.

If Texas wants a highly educated and skilled workforce it must make better use of technology to reduce costs. Once again, those who attend institutions of higher education are hit with both the amount of taxes they pay, the cost of goods they buy as a consumer that are taxed, and the direct expenditures to the institutions they attend. Anything we as policy makers can do to lessen that burden should and must be done if we are to continue to attract business and experience continued economic prosperity.

Recommendations

Economic Development

- Texas should re-organize the State Economic Development Commission and the Texas Department of Economic Development; and,
- Texas should focus on non-incentive measures to encourage economic development.

Secondary Education

- Texas should remove the statutory cap on the number of charter schools that are allowed;
- Texas should remove regulations that prevent school districts from removing ineffective teachers and properly compensating the most effective teachers;
- Texas should allow traditional public schools to operate under the same rules and regulations as charter schools;
- Texas should develop career based curriculums and make career counseling and aptitude testing a priority;
- Texas should evaluate the use of the Preliminary Scholastic Assessment Test/National Merit Scholarship Qualifying Test and/or the PLAN tests to measure achievement in English, math, reading, and science in 10th grade students;
- Texas should evaluate the use of the SAT and ACT tests to evaluate college readiness;
- Texas should develop and fully fund a short intervention tutorial program for students in need of remedial education;
- Texas should create a task force to identify the cost of providing an efficient and equitable education on a per student basis;
- Texas should reexamine the need for the many reports, and regulations it imposes on local independent school

districts and determine a cost benefit analysis to justify its conclusions;

- The legislature should consider utilizing a block grant funding approach when providing state monies to local districts to equalize the amount spent on educating children;
- Texas should require publishers to provide primary and secondary education textbooks in a format compatible with common electronic reading devices; and,
- Texas should update the weights used to determine funding levels.

Higher Education

- Institutions of higher education should move more classes online;
- The state should create and fully fund a Texas Open Source Digital Library; and, Institutions of higher education should digitize libraries.

Supplement To

TEXAS
TOMORROW

Texas Should Move to Priority Based Budgeting

Background

As governments at all levels struggle to meet basic needs with ever more limited resources, policy makers seek new ways to balance budgets without raising taxes. Economists agree that higher taxes do not spur economic growth and they understand that stalled economic growth limits revenue available to policy makers. And deciding how to spend that revenue, or what the state wants to "buy," has become more important than ever.

Taxpayers, now more than ever, are demanding to know not only how their money is being spent but how policy makers are making those decisions. Those questions have led to a call for greater transparency of government spending as well as a call for greater transparency of the decision making process that precedes spending decisions.

Priority based budgeting (PBB) is a method of setting priorities that provides transparency, accountability, and a method of top down funding that families must use every day.

Understanding the Texas budget process

States use a variety of methods to create their budget such as zero based budgeting, program based budgeting, budget by strategy, and performance based budgeting just to name a few. Up until the mid-1970's Texas budget was based on object of expense which told policy makers what the money was spent on but not where it was spent. In the mid 70's the state moved to program budgeting which told policy makers where tax dollars were being spent but not how they were spent. Then in 1991 Texas moved to performance based budgeting which told policy makers how the money was being spent and tied agency performance to the budget. In that year agencies were required to develop strategic plans so policy makers could gauge the performance of state agencies. While the current system is not perfect, it does position Texas to move to the next stage of its budget evolution, doing a cost-benefit analysis of the programs that the budget supports.

Throughout this evolution, the Texas budget has lacked one critical element, a clear set of priorities based on the core functions of government. So budget writers have no guide as to what is important to the taxpayer.

Priority Based Budgeting

Priority based budgeting is a simple concept that forces a state to deal with complex issues. It has helped states and local governments across the county balance budgets and close gaps between available revenue and spending needs. It relieves the pressure from special interest on budget writers and policy makers to fund programs that may or may not be what the taxpayer sees as a function of government.

In each of the past three or four sessions of the legislature, the Governor has asked state agencies to cut spending by ten percent with few exceptions. What if a different question was asked? What if the process started with, "How should we spend the money we have?"

A priority based budget forces budget writers and policy makers to decide what is really important and what types of things government should really be doing. Is the funding of the Cosmetology Commission a necessary function of government? What about the funding of insurance programs?

Anatomy of a Priority Based Budget

There are four fundamental questions that must be answered in any PBB system.

1. What is the role of government?
2. How much revenue will the state have to spend?
3. What are the essential services government must provide to fulfill its purpose?
4. How will we know if government is doing a good job?

Texas is well positioned to move toward PBB because it already answers two of the four questions. The Comptroller of Public Accounts is required to issue a revenue forecast and to certify that any budget passed by the Legislature will not exceed available revenues. These revenue estimates have been very accurate over the years and have served that purpose quite well. And as previously mentioned, since 1991 state agencies have been required to develop strategic plans and budget writers have attached performance measures to those plans. That information is provided to policy makers for their use in determining funding levels for the strategies submitted by those agencies.

The third question concerning necessary essential services can only be answered after the core functions of government are identified.

Advantages

The one clear advantage to utilizing a PBB is the elimination of agency silo effects and the overwhelming pressure from special interests. That leaves budget writers and policy makers free to examine the effectiveness of programs rather than deciding the policy benefits of a program.

Another benefit is that regardless of the budget method used, policy makers have a clear set of goals to guide them and a clear understanding of the taxpayer's wishes. That allows them to concentrate on how to spend revenue and not on what to spend revenue which may take much of the politics out of budgeting.

Setting Priorities

Setting priorities will not be easy because Texas operates under an outdated and inflexible constitution. Additionally, 80 percent of the revenue the state spends is dedicated either by constitution, statute, or federal programs. Unless that is resolved it will be difficult for policy makers to fund core functions to their fullest.

Where to Look

One place to start would be in the constitution. But that is not as easy as it seems, especially in Texas. Public engagement can be used to directly identify the wishes of the taxpayer and there are efforts in other states and local governments that Texas policy makers may look to for examples.

That is not to say the constitution does not give direction as to what government's priorities should be. For instance, for as far back as Spanish and French rule education has been thought to be a priority of government. All other priorities followed.

Other ideas can be found in the many amendments to the constitution. For instance, many amendments dedicated funds for one purpose or another or limited spending on some items. For example Article 3, section 51-a limits state spending on assistance to needy children and their caretakers to no more than one percent of the total state budget (not including federal matching funds and administrative costs) while revenue for Texas' highways is protected by the constitution.

Citizen Input

Citizens are calling for transparency in government because they feel disenfranchised from the process. One thing the Texas Constitution makes perfectly clear is that all government power comes from the people. And using a strategy to seek public input into the core functions of government will empower citizens and increase their participation in government.

Other States

Other states and local units of government have used PBB to successfully close gaps between revenues and expenditures. In each case a focused attempt to identify the core functions of government was necessary. In 2003, Washington State utilized PBB to fully close a $2.8 billion deficit without raising taxes.[19]

Recommendations

A. Texas should implement priority based budgeting.

As previously discussed, priority based budgeting treats all of state government as a single enterprise. New programs are evaluated on the basis of how they contribute to the strategies used to achieve the state's priorities, or core functions. This combined with zero based budgeting will help Texas continue to be an example of economic excellence in the face of extreme economic challenges. To do that, state policy makers must first identify the core functions of government.

B. The Texas Legislature should form a statewide citizen-legislature commission to identify and prioritize the core functions of government.

Utilizing a strategy of public engagement, policy makers can identify the functions of government wanted by those who pay for it. Citizen involvement will flourish when included in that process.

A plan should be developed to utilize technology to gather public comment. A series of meetings should be held in different regions of the state in which public engagement is utilized to engage stake holders at all levels including local units of government. The commission should be made up of representatives from all sectors of the economy, the Texas House, the Texas Senate, and stakeholders from the different regions in Texas to ensure the broadest representation possible. It may be necessary to establish regional task forces in a structure similar to the regional water planning groups that report the statewide commission which will then compiles the information and present a final report to the legislature for consideration.

C. The Texas Legislative Budget Board in concert with the Texas Department of Information Resources should develop a web based interactive website to seek input into what the citizens feel the priorities of government should be.

Every Texan pays taxes in one form or another and should be allowed the opportunity to have a say in how their tax dollars are spent. Information technology has, for the first time, presented policy makers with a tool to seek and evaluate citizen input into what the priorities of government should be. The development of an interactive website would not only enable citizens the opportunity to provide such input but it could also present citizens with the opportunity to show policy makers how they would balance the state budget.

The Texas Budget Process
Should Be Modified

Summary

The Texas budget process has been an ever evolving process incorporating the best practices of the times. Currently Texas uses a performance based budgeting system that incorporates state agency strategic planning. While effective, the system needs to be updated and improved upon. Modern technology and data gathering and analysis methods have made more information available to policy makers and budget writers. Economic conditions have resulted in the taxpayer's call for transparency, efficiency, and more effective use of tax dollars.

Modern budgeting incorporates more than allocating money to programs based on a programs ability to meet its performance measures. It now must allocate funds based on core functions of government, and whether or not a program provides a return for the investment the taxpayer makes in it. While the current process serves Texas well, it can be modified and improved upon to provide better and more meaningful information to policy makers.

As Texas faces difficult economic times policy makers must make better decisions and have a process in place that provides timely and accurate information.

Background

Texas like many other states was hit hard by the recent economic downturn due to an increased demand of services and a reduction of revenues to meet those needs. Policy makers were also faced with the fact that Texas is a balanced budget state. No expenditures beyond projected available revenues can be spent. Two sessions ago it used Federal stimulus money to balance its budget but that one time infusion of cash only delayed the inevitable realization that balancing succeeding budgets would take fiscal restraint and in many cases creative accounting.

Budget Principles

Early in 2012, Governor Rick Perry proposed his Texas Budget Compact, "a collection of five common-sense principles that should guide the direction of the legislature in the upcoming session and sessions to come."[20] Soon after the Governor issued his Texas Budget Compact he and the Texas Legislative Budget Board issued their budget instructions to state agencies, boards, appellate courts and institutions of higher education. These instructions are the first step in the development of the Texas budget.

The instructions directed agencies to use the funds expended in Fiscal Year (FY) 2012 and budgeted in FY 2013 (current levels) as the baseline for their legislative appropriations requests. Agencies were also asked to submit a "supplemental schedule detailing how they would reduce the baseline request by an additional 10 percent (in 5 percent increments) in General Revenue Funds and General Revenue Dedicated Funds."[21]

Better questions to ask

For the third budget cycle in a row, state leaders have begun the process by ordering across the board cuts or holding spending to past biennium levels that had suffered from across the board cuts. But across the board cuts are not the answer. While they may seem equitable and avoid conflict, they are not strategic and do nothing to shape and size government. Nor do they create value for taxpayers. In some ways they represent an abdication of the legislature's responsibility to appropriate state revenues. There are better questions for policy makers to ask. But the current system does not provide the necessary guidance or information.

For instance, the question, "Is that program effective?" is a fundamentally different question than, "is that program worthwhile?"[22] Additionally, rather than ask what should be cut, policy makers should ask, "On what do we want to spend the taxpayer's dollars?"

Texas Budget Process

States use a variety of methods to create their budget such as zero based budgeting, program based budgeting, budget by strategy, and performance based budgeting just to name a few. Up until the mid-1970's Texas budget was based on object of expense which told policy makers what the money was spent on but not where it was spent. In the mid 70's the state moved to program budgeting which told policy makers where tax dollars were being spent but not how they were spent. Then in 1991 Texas moved to performance based budgeting which told policy makers how the money was being spent and tied agency performance to the budget. In that year agencies were required to develop strategic plans so policy makers could gauge the performance of state agencies. While the current system is not perfect, it does position Texas to move to the next stage of its budget evolution. However, to get there some things need to change.

Next Steps

The legislature needs to decide on what it wants to spend the money taxpayers provide. Moving to a priority based budget would be the next step in budgetary evolution in Texas. A priority based budget would provide policy makers with a clear set of priorities based on what citizens decide are the core functions of government. But even with that there are things that must be done to the budget itself to make it all work.

Measuring performance

Texas has done a good job in developing performance measures, but there are weaknesses in the system. The problem is that under performance does not translate into budget cuts. The most glaring weakness of the system is that agencies themselves set their performance measures. While they do so with the advice of the Governor's Office of Budget, Planning, and Policy and the Legislative Budget Board they do so without that clear direction provided in a priority based system. And meeting performance targets is also made more difficult when considering federally funded program requirements which can set up dual reporting requirements. This can be confusing and cause agencies an undue amount of time and expense in reporting on their performance. The process may be further complicated by potential disagreements between systems which generate problems and issues that would not exist had the systems been synchronized and coordinated. And finally, one of the biggest holes in the Texas performance system is the lack of any measure for functions of indirect administration even though they are relatively consistent across agencies.[23] This is especially curious since administration can account for up to 30 percent of an agency's budget.

Recommendations

A. Texas should reexamine its budget process to ensure that it provides policy makers and budget writers with the information necessary for them to make informed decisions regarding program funding.

Information and how that information is presented to policy makers and budget writers are key to their ability to make wise spending decisions. The incorporation of outcomes and cost-benefit analyses would be a step in the right direction.

B. Require state agencies to include information about how they plan to evaluate the effectiveness of their programs and link their disbursements to evidence.

Currently, agencies are only required to align their programs to their strategic plans without mention as to how they plan to evaluate a program's effectiveness based on the cost of the program. Requiring a cost-benefit analysis of programs would be a step in the right direction.

C. Incorporate zero based budgeting into process.

Zero based budgeting will require a closer examination of every dollar spent by Texas government. In 2003 Texas used this to close a multibillion dollar gap by requiring agencies to justify every dollar in their Legislative Appropriations Request. It has not been used since.

It's Time for Cost-benefit Analysis of State Spending

Summary

Texas policy makers and budget writers should make use of a tool that every business uses when deciding on where it directs its resources and on what it spends its money using cost-benefit analyses which have been around for decades in business and have been used in government for the past 15 years beginning with the State of Washington. The idea is spreading to other states as well. These analyses have reduced budget expenditures and helped policy makers direct funding to programs that provide benefit to the taxpayer. The Texas Legislative Budget Board has assigned a team of analysts to work with the Pew Center for the States' Results First project to assess the costs and benefits of policy options and use that data to make decisions based on results in the area of criminal justice spending. The LBB should apply this principle to existing programs as well as new programs.

Background

While measuring agency performance, Texas' budget does not present policy makers with the cost-benefit information they need to assess the value of a program when weighed against its costs. But there is an answer: a cost-benefit analysis can be used to evaluate the desirability of a given program. It will help answer the question of whether a program is worthwhile. This system helps policy makers rank programs according to their effectiveness at achieving desired results. This will ensure that vital services are being funded before less critical ones. And when funding programs, policy makers can start at the top of the list and appropriate dollars until they run out.

Washington State has been using this method for the last 15 years to great success. Currently, a team at the Texas Legislative Budget Board is working with the Pew Center on the States' Results First project to develop a research and analysis model that will provide such a cost-benefit analysis tool to Texas policy makers. The model will include:

- an analysis of all available research;
- a calculation of the potential return on investment of policy options;
- a prediction of the investment risk;
- a ranking of the projected benefits, costs, and risks;
- an identification of ineffective programs;
- and, an assessment of the combined benefits and costs of a portfolio of policies.

The team is developing the model to examine the state's investment in our criminal justice system. The results of such an analysis and model can be substantial. Using such a model Washington State decided to invest in crime prevention and treatment programs that saved $1.3 billion over a two year budget cycle and decreased crime rates and juvenile-arrest rates.[24]

Recommendations

A. The Texas Legislature should direct the Legislative Budget Board to design a pilot program that provides a cost-benefit analysis of existing state funded Criminal Justice Programs and provide adequate resources for that project.

Using programs now being funded in the appropriations bills the LBB should identify the elements necessary to analyze the cost versus benefit of those programs. One example is the cost of programs that provide health care to those incarcerated in state facilities. The current project is trying to identify the total cost of criminal justice in Texas including both local and state costs. But that may not be needed for an analysis of state expenditures. To help in its project, the LBB should have the support of the Department of Criminal Justice, The Texas Judicial Council, The Comptroller of Public Accounts, The Juvenile Justice Commission, The Texas Youth Commission, The Texas Board of Pardons and paroles, The Texas Department of Public Safety, The Correctional Managed Health Care Committee, and the Texas Department of Information Resources for data gathering and analysis system input.

B. The Legislative Budget Board should be encouraged to identify other areas of government spending that would benefit from a cost benefit analysis of program effectiveness.

Much of state spending is not driven by outcomes but by performance. Even then the measures do not reflect the benefit society receives from this spending. Without such information policy makers cannot legitimately prioritize the programs that deserve funding. Other areas of interest would be child welfare, pre-K-12 education, adult and children's mental health, and substance abuse.

Rethinking Regulation in Texas

Summary

There is no doubt that government regulation is needed, but there is doubt that the degree to which government regulates is truly necessary. There is also question as to how those regulations are carried out, especially the permitting that they require. Identifying the many regulations that businesses operate under and taxpayers pay for is like peeling an onion. One finds layer after layer of them. Identifying the true cost of those regulations is no less difficult. There is much that can be done to lessen the regulatory burden on businesses and to lessen the costs to taxpayers and consumers.

Background

Everything is regulated by government from the mattresses we sleep on to the air we breathe. While many regulations are understood to be necessary, many more are unnecessary or have outlived their usefulness. The growth of the regulated community is in direct response to politicians pandering to special interest groups with little regard to the outcomes of their actions. In Texas, that problem is exacerbated by the fact that the Legislature meets only 5 months every two years and must give agencies, boards, commissions and department's great leeway in regulation enforcement and permit creation. This is done through administrative rulemaking.

The number of regulations drives the cost both to government and the economy. Costs whether incurred by government or business is ultimately borne by the consumer and taxpayer. And these costs can be enormous. It has been estimated that in 2004 complying with federal regulations cost businesses $648 billion, or $5,633 per employee.[25] While recent data is not available it is reasonable to assume that cost has risen above $1 trillion during the intervening 8 years. In Texas, the Texas Department of Licensing and Regulation has more than doubled its staff since 1999 due to the increase in the number of statutes it enforces and the number of licensees it oversees. But the total cost to the taxpayer for development, managing, and enforcing regulations is not known and the data needed to determine such is nonexistent in Texas.

While many of the regulations Texas businesses must face are federal, the state can reduce the burden to those businesses by being smarter about how it regulates. For instance a dry cleaner is required to pay a yearly $2,000 fee with to Texas Commission on Environmental Quality in case of ground contamination due to a chemical spill. That dry cleaner could purchase a $1,000 insurance policy that would provide much more coverage than $2,000 if remediation is needed. Another example of the problem is getting permits needed to construct an industrial plant. Many projects require local, state, and federal permits. The most onerous are required by the Clean Air Act, and some require multiple state and federal permits. The cost of these lay not only in the consultants and staff time devoted to navigating these regulations, but in the delay of construction. Texas has a model in place that can cut the wait time down while meeting state and federal regulation requirements.

If Texas is going to continue its economic growth and provide needed jobs it must take action to reduce the regulatory burden on business and industry.

Recommendations

A. A state task force should be established to identify all regulations and permits and study their effectiveness, usefulness, and impacts on the economy and government spending with a focus on those that are 10 years old and older.

There has never been a meaningful mechanism by which regulations and permits are reviewed once they are passed and enacted. Most agency performance measures are geared toward the number of licenses or permits issued or the number of regulatory actions taken. Sometimes it is only the number of inspections conducted. No economic impact is done and nor is a review done of the effectiveness or continued need for the regulation or permit. The legislature should appoint a statewide task force to examine the need for existing regulations and permits. It should also work to determine the true cost to the Texas economy of complying and enforcing those regulations.

B. The Legislature should direct the Office of State-Federal Relations to engage the Texas Congressional delegation to encourage federal regulatory agencies to work with Texas regulatory agencies to align regulatory and permitting requirements.

One problem with permitting is that federal and state agencies argue over jurisdiction when enforcing permitting requirements. This causes delays in projects which increases costs to the developers. State and federal regulatory agencies should work together to align their requirements to eliminate this problem.

C. The legislature should expand the concept of the Coastal Coordination Council to all permits required of businesses operating in Texas.

The Coastal Coordination Council model was designed to streamline the permitting process and cut delays in project construction due to that process. The Council oversees a program that requires state permitting agencies to align their permitting requirements so that a project doesn't have to comply with competing requirements. It also provides a mechanism by which a developer can submit its plan to the Council and receive an assurance that the plan meets the various permitting requirements. This allows the developer to begin project development while obtaining the necessary permits.

D. The Legislature should require a cost-benefit analysis of any regulation or permit required by statute or administrative rule before that statute or rule is adopted.

Currently there is no established mechanism to weigh the cost to the public of a regulation against the expected public benefits. This is information that policy makers should have when deciding on the imposition of a regulation on Texas businesses.

Texas Agencies Should Improve Back Office Efficiency

Summary

Governments at all levels are constantly working to become more efficient in an effort to save tax dollars and better serve its citizens. It is not uncommon for state agencies to identify private sector best practices that would achieve these goals. The Texas legislature directed the Texas Workforce Commission to conduct a pilot project using one of these methods, commonly referred to as Lean Six Sigma. According to an agency report to the legislature the pilot project was a complete success.

Background

For a number of years industrial sector businesses have employed a method of improving quality and reducing the costs of services called Lean Six Sigma. While developed for manufacturing processes, its principles can be applied to many business processes that deliver a product to a customer. In 2011 I helped author and pass S.B. 563 which directed the Texas Workforce Commission to, "to establish a pilot program to improve the efficiency and quality of operations while reducing costs, and to adopt a structured approach for identifying the wasteful use of state resources and improving processes."[26]

The agency selected its Work Opportunity Tax Credit program for the pilot project and applied the Integrated Theory of Constraints Lean Six Sigma methodology to increase the number of applications processed and reduce the amount of time it took to process employer applications. The pilot program was a complete success. The program realized an increase in productivity (increased the number of determinations, and decreased turnaround time), an increase in benefits to employers (in the amount of $97 million), and a reduction of costs to the state (50% per determination). And it did so, within existing resources and without increasing staffing or procuring automation."[27] All of this resulted in more people put to work in Texas and more quickly.

Recommendations

A. Texas agencies, boards, and commissions should employ the Integrated Theory of Constraints Lean Six Sigma methodology to improve back office operations.

Not all agency programs are appropriate for this type of management tool. Those that involve processes resulting in the delivery of a product to citizens may be the type and should be examined first. The Council on Competitive Government should enter into a consulting agreement with a firm experienced in the development of such programs to work with state agencies to identify programs that would benefit from such methodology.

The State Should Utilize Statewide Building Maintenance Services Contracts

Summary

Currently, Texas spends over $40 million annually on building maintenance services. Each agency uses multiple vendors for each trade service. It is estimated that Texas would save 10%, or $4 million per year, by changing the procurement process. The state has a mechanism available to purchase these services from a single vendor and have that contract managed by a centralized entity.

Background

In 2010, the State of Texas spent over $40 million for Building & maintenance expenses. These expenses included repair for elevators, windows, doors, overhead doors, painting and carpentry. The process for securing such work is repeated by each agency for each maintenance item needed. This is a costly and cumbersome process. It is estimated that securing a contract can cost up to $2,000 and issuing purchase orders under that contract can cost hundreds of dollars. The current system also lacks economies of scale.

The state created the Council on Competitive Government to avoid just these kinds of expenses when services are found to be common among agencies. The Council first must determine a service to be a "statewide service." It will then design a contract and select a vendor to be used on behalf of all state agencies. The agencies will still be responsible for issuing work orders and paying for the services rendered, but the council will manage the overall contract. The council could utilize the Texas Facilities Commission as the central intake point for all agency maintenance work orders and then issue the work order to the vendor for completion.

Recommendations

A. The Council on Competitive Government (CCG) should declare the maintenance of facilities as a statewide service and issue a contract for such service.

The legislature should direct the CCG to declare that building maintenance services be considered a statewide service and issue a vendor contract accordingly.

B. The Texas Facilities Commission (TFC) should develop a web based automated system to be used by state agencies when maintenance is needed.

TFC should develop an automated web based solution for all state agencies to use requesting and completing maintenance work orders. These agencies should first explore modification of legacy systems before the purchase of a new system to handle this task.

Texas Should Rethink Its Economic Development Strategy

Summary

Most economic development in Texas is conducted at the local level. The state supports that effort through various state agencies and the Department of Economic Development and Tourism within the office of the Governor. It alone oversees more than 67 different programs. In 2011 the Texas Legislature formed the Select Committee on Economic Development to review state economic development programs and make recommendations to the Legislature, including whether or not to consolidate the programs or have one agency in charge of economic development.

At a recent meeting of the Select Committee on Economic Development, one of the committee's subcommittee chairmen was reported to have said that, "he has heard criticism that the Texas diversified approach can be confusing or slow down the recruitment process."[28] Witnesses told the committee that other challenges to economic development in Texas exist in education, transportation, water, health care and increasing competition from other states.

As competition drives the cost of luring business and manufacturing to the state the cost may at some point become prohibitive for the taxpayer to support. At that point Texas must be able to offer other things businesses find attractive.

Background

The Texas Department of Economic Development was formed in 1997 as an outgrowth of the Texas Department of Commerce. The new agency was tasked with the Texas Smart Jobs Program and tourism as well as economic development duties. It suffered through a number of mismanagement issues and in 2003 it was restructured and moved to the office of the Governor. It was thought that it would be more effective there as it coordinated economic development activities across the many state agencies that played a key role in the state's economic development. Others thought the move would give the Governor too much authority over economic development for Texas.

Since that move the state's economic development process has been mired in and threatened by politics. It has also been viewed as confusing and slow to recruit new jobs.

A group of Cornell researchers found that factors such as skilled labor, strong infrastructure and good schools offer more incentive for businesses to start up or relocate. They also found that, "tax abatement subsidies to individual firms do not significantly impact firm decisions to relocate or expand."[29]

If Texas wants to compete for businesses and good jobs in the future, it must present a less complicated and coordinated effort in attracting those businesses. It must also provide a solid infrastructure of good roads, power and water as well as an educated workforce. And finally it must present a clear and reliable system of awarding incentives that is deemed as fair and above the appearance of political cronyism.

Recommendations

A. Texas should recreate the State Economic Development Commission and the Texas Department of Economic Development.

A new agency should be created to undertake the economic development duties of the various agencies and the Economic Development and Tourism Department of the Office of the

Governor while leaving tourism with the Governor's office. It should focus on business expansion and relocation prospects, with the goal of developing job creation and export opportunities for Texas. It should also offer permitting and licensing assistance similar to the work of the Coastal Conservation Council. And it should assist local governments in their economic development efforts.

B. Texas should focus on non-incentive measures to encourage economic development.

If Texas is to compete nationally and globally for new business investments it must provide a first rate infrastructure and a highly educated and skilled workforce. It must address its transportation infrastructure such as roads, ports, and airports. It must make its secondary and higher educational systems first rate. It must also offer a stable tax system. And finally it must provide an adequate supply of water and energy to business.

Reforming Public Education in Texas

Summary

The Texas Constitution calls for an efficient system of public education, but the writers of the 1876 constitution recognized, as Texas courts have stated, that efficiency is not limited to the financing of education. It is now clear that the quality of education was as important then as it is now. In every decision the Texas Supreme Court has issued on school finance the court advised that the issue of quality was as important as finance and repeatedly stated that the quality of the system should be addressed as well.

While the constitution calls for public education, it does not say it has to be owned by the state. Rather it seems that the Texas legislature has recognized that fact when it allowed the use of charter schools and home-rule school districts. There is no doubt that much can still be done to improve the quality of education. Of equal importance is the need to stem the tide of children dropping out of high school.

But only fundamental changes in the quality of education and the way we educate our children will solve these issues.

Background

While the Texas Constitution guarantees an "efficient system of public free schools,"[30] it has been acknowledged that efficiency has two components: finance, and quality. Traditionally, quality has been viewed as tied to the amount money spent it, but in reality they are mutually exclusive. One does not, and should not, depend upon the other.

Over the years the courts have had one consistent message to policy makers; that efficiency goes beyond money. While the courts have been asked to rule on the equitableness of the finance system each has taken the opportunity to point out that money is not the only issue or the only solution. That is until now.

The pleading in Fort Bend Independent School District, et al.[31] has asked the court to now rule on the qualitative component of "efficiency," as the writers of the 1876 constitution intended. This pleading points out that the Supreme Court of Texas had repeatedly called for qualitative change, or how education is delivered.

System ownership

Who should "own" the public school system in Texas? While the writers of the 1876 constitution followed suit with previous constitutions and called for a free and efficient public school system, they did not say the state had to own the system. Because subsequent legislatures built the system they also, by default, claimed ownership of the system. Only in recent times have policymakers realized that for profit entities could deliver quality education without the need for state built facilities and undue regulation.

The other problem with state ownership of public schools has been the influence of special interests groups in defining what public education should look like. These pressures have also politicized the practice of educating Texas children beyond what was envisioned in 1876 or even necessary today. Debates over curriculum have resulted in silencing alternative views even when necessary for understanding. That is evident in the Texas Republican Party's platform which seems opposed to critical thinking and calls for knowledge-based education. Knowledge-based education is just a new name for outcome based learning which is more about social engineering than it is education. Can this devolve into teaching children what we want them to know rather than teaching them to think about what is taught? It's the difference between knowing that the sun rises in the east and knowing why it does so.

Chipping away at change

Recent years have seen many changes in the delivery system of education in Texas. The allowance of charter schools, home rule school districts, and home schooling has changed the educational system landscape in Texas. While that is true, more can and must be done if Texas is to achieve the vision of those who drafted and adopted the 1876. Better utilization of these non-traditional forms of public education will likely benefit students, taxpayers, and eventually the Texas economy.

One of the elements lacking in the public school system is an effective way of dealing with the high rate of dropouts in secondary education. There has also been a drive toward preparing students for college rather than preparing them for careers. While programs have developed for students wanting work rather than college, it has been localized to specific school districts or even selected campuses.

Addressing the substantial drop out rate in Texas schools

Texas has done much to address the issue of students dropping out of high school but more can be done. Students drop out of school for many reasons and there is no one solution to the problem. But the system itself contributes to the problem. Our schools are geared toward readying students for four-year degree programs. While every student should have some post-secondary education, not every student wants to or should go to college. For example, it is a well-known fact that there is a shortage of skilled tradesmen and women in Texas. This is due the fact that Texas public education has for many years focused on teaching a student how to design a car rather than providing the training and education to teach someone who to build or repair it.

Providing career based curriculums to students may be one way to keep students in school. The student who wants to be a welder does not need the same math education as one who wants to be an economist and the economist doesn't need the same math that a theoretical physicist would need. For some students a class of pool playing will provide all the geometry and physics they'll need in their lifetime if handled properly. Besides, there is no reason education can't be fun. The reality is that these curriculums will not be successful if students do not know what they want to or have the ability to do. Career counseling and aptitude testing has taken a back seat lately as schools have had to tighten their financial belts and prepare their students to take the standardized testing that has become so popular with policy makers. Helping our children realize their potential and decide what they want to do in life should be one of the top goals in secondary education.

Recommendations

A. Remove the statutory cap on the number of charter schools that are allowed.

The number of charter schools is capped by statute at 215 which prevents new charter operators from moving into the Texas market. The test scores of current charter schools are on par, or better, than those of traditional public schools. It is estimated that there are 56,000 students on charter school waiting lists.[32]

B. Remove regulations that prevent school districts from removing ineffective teachers and properly compensating the most effective teachers.

Minimum teacher salary schedules and long term contracts are not in the best interest of the students or the taxpayer. The process to remove ineffective teachers is arduous at best and it makes it difficult for schools to manage personnel budgets. Schools should be able to reward effective teachers and remove ineffective ones. No business would keep "dead wood" on its payroll and survive for very long and schools shouldn't be made to do so. Allow the local taxpayers and parents to decide if the school did the right thing when letting a teacher go.

C. Allow traditional public schools to operate under the same rules and regulations as charter schools.

This would make the system less arbitrary and more efficient resulting in enormous savings for traditional public school systems. If operating under fewer regulations was considered good enough for charter schools, it should be good enough for traditional public schools. Local taxpayers and parents can let the district know the information they want and can decide locally if they want to spend the money and district's time in producing it.

F. Develop career based curriculums and make career counseling and aptitude testing a priority.

Anything we can do to help students decide what they can and want to do to make a living should be encouraged as early as possible. As mentioned earlier if we only gear our students for four-year degrees we are shortchanging our economic future. What good is it for us to teach someone to design a car if there is no one who can repair it?

It's Time to Rethink Standardized Testing

Summary

Since the inception of standardized testing in 1980 Texas has spent billions on the program but still remains near the bottom of all states on many education rankings. The tests have turned from a diagnostic tool to assess student performance to a system that is punitive in nature now being used to measure the effectiveness of schools and school districts. There are better and less costly ways to make sure our students are prepared for college and it's time that Texas explores those options.

Background

Texans spend $56 billion dollars on public education and yet the state ranks near the bottom when compared to other states in a number of important categories. It ranks 49th in performance on the verbal SAT and 46th in math, 43rd in the percent of students graduating from high school, and 43rd in per student spending. Added to that is the fact that 31% of students entering higher education directly from high school require remediation. To be fair though, Texas faces some major hurdles. Sixteen percent of its students are designated as Limited English students, and 55 percent of all students are considered economically disadvantaged.

As dismal as these statistics are, they are not a surprise. As far back as the mid 1990's policy makers were aware that the remediation problem existed and was getting worse. The Texas Comptroller of Public Accounts recommended holding public secondary schools accountable for the basic skills of their graduates entering college. In that policy recommendation it was noted that "students in secondary schools have been required to take examinations testing basic skills as a graduation requirement since 1985."[33] That was approximately 10 years prior to the writing of the recommendation. Almost thirty years later the state is still wrestling with the same problem.

Enter Standardized Testing

Because of Texas' student performance, when measured against other states and nations, and the increasing cost of public education taxpayers urged lawmakers to develop a system that would evaluate whether they were getting their money's worth. So policy makers rushed into standardized testing. The first, The Texas Assessment of Basic Skills, test was administered in the 1979-1980 school year and measured student performance in mathematics, reading and writing for students in grades 3, 5 and 9."[34]

Table 1 lists the standardized tests used in Texas over the years.

Test	Years administered		Grades	Notes
Texas Assessment of Basic Skills (TABS)	1979-1985	Math, reading and writing	3, 5, 9	
Texas Educational Assessment of Minimum Skills (TEAMS)	1985-1990	Math, reading and writing	3, 5, 7, 9	
Texas Educational Assessment of Minimum Skills (TEAMS)	1985-1990	Math, English language arts	11	Passage required for graduation.
Texas Assessment of Academic Skills (TAAS)	1990-2002	Academic skills with an emphasis on problem-solving and critical thinking skills.	3, 5, 7, 9, 11	Passage in 11th grade required for graduation; science and social studies added in 1994. 4 und-of-course exams were added at the high school level.

Texas Assessment of Knowledge and Skills (TAKS)	2003-2011	Math, English language arts, science and social studies	3 through 11	Promotion in grades 3, 5 and 8 are tied to test results.
State of Texas Assessments of Academic Readiness (STARR)	2012	Math, English language arts, science and social studies	3 through 8	More rigorous than TAKS.
State of Texas Assessments of Academic Readiness (STARR)	2012	Algebra I, geometry, Algebra II, biology, chemistry, physics, English I, English II, English III, world geography, world history, and U.S. history	9 through 12	Replaces grade-specific assessments with 12 end-of-course assessment. Passage is required for graduation

Table 1. Standardized testing in Texas

Many think that testing has gotten out of hand due to the number of tests students must now take. Others believe that testing is not a good gauge of student learning and is not a good way of assessing the effectiveness of our schools in teaching students. There are those who believe the tests are flawed and that they cost too much and put too much pressure on students. Even legislative leaders think the stakes are too high and put too much pressure on students and teachers. But the drive for accountability has been augmented by a multi-billion dollar industry hungry for public education dollars.

How Much Does It Cost

The state contracted with NCS Pearson Inc., the nation's largest testing company, to develop, administer and grade the State's STARR test. That contract is worth $500 million dollars through 2015. By 2015 the state will have paid Pearson nearly $1.2 billion for developing standardized tests and related materials since 2000.[35] In 2012 the cost is $90 million and expected to be near $100 million in 2015.

But that is not the only cost of these tests. In 2004 the state signed a $17.7 million four year deal with Grow Network for study guides designed for high school students that didn't pass the TAKS test. The state also purchased summer remediation study guides from Pearson at the cost of $8.8 million for the period from 2006 through 2011.[36]

Districts across the state have reported spending millions in local district funds to administer the tests. Because of the number of tests some schools have had to hire test administrators. They've had to hire additional part time teachers or teacher aides to monitor hallways and bathrooms. And administrators must spend time reading, "a 156-page manual, plus a 47-page security supplement, to prepare for a testing season that runs from October through July."[37]

> Pearson's North American Education division, which last year reported sales of £2.6 billion British pounds ($4.03 billion) and an operating profit of €493 million pounds, up 5 percent from 2010, designs tests for many U.S. states and scores hundreds of millions of standardized exams each year.
>
> *Simon, Stephanie, "Parents protest surge in standardized testing" Reuters 06/12/12*

Is It Working

"During the 2002-03 school year, the TEA administered 60 separate standardized tests. This year, Zyskowski says, the number will be 138."[38]

Business organizations have entered the debate over school accountability citing the low graduation rates and need for remedial education is an indication of a poorly educated work force. These groups have dug their feet in the ground calling on legislators to not put more money into the system until things improve. But the State's chief job officer, Texas Workforce Commissioner Tom Pauken, has called for the elimination of standardized testing saying that it short changes employers by teaching to the test instead of focusing on real learning. Just retired Education Commissioner Robert Scott also called for a reduction in the emphasis on standardized testing.

As previously mentioned, Texas ranks nationally towards the bottom in key educational statistics. Also, a third of students graduating from high school are unprepared for college. And the number of drops outs is alarming. It would seem that escalating number of standardized tests to assess college readiness and school accountability has not worked. In fact it may have exacerbated the drop out problem. At-risk students are more likely to drop out after failing the TAKS and/or STAAR tests feeling they just aren't good enough to make the grade.

Supporters of the high stakes standardized tests argue that it is the only way to make sure districts are spending tax dollars efficiently. The problem is that since no one knows exactly how school districts spend their money no academic test can accurately measure efficiency. Aside from that standardized testing has turned from a diagnostic tool to a punitive exercise. These tests measure neither college readiness nor efficiency in spending. For one reason the tests may have been flawed in their design.

It was interesting to note the scores on the recently administered STAAR tests. Students scored better in math, biology, and geography than they did in reading comprehension. One has to ask the question, "If they can't read how can they pass anything else?" As it turns out the test design may be flawed. A recent study released by University of Texas at Austin professor Walter Stroup came to the conclusion that because of the design of the tests, "they are virtually useless at measuring the effects of classroom instruction."[39]

There are Alternatives

There are alternatives to standardized testing. The state has spent billions of dollars developing its own set of tests to assess college readiness and to hold schools accountable for the money they spend. But not much has changed with all of that money spent on testing. Students are still not prepared for college, they still drop out, and the education system itself has not been improved.

Perhaps it is time to disassociate measuring college readiness and assessing financial accountability. No test of student achievement is a true measure of the effectiveness of our educational system. There are too many variables involved to hold teachers accountable for a student's success or failure. But there are tools the state can use to assess a student's readiness for college. And other states are using those tools. Both the PSAT and the pre-ACT tests can be effective tools for measuring preparedness in the sophomore and junior years. And since most students don't need full course instructions to be prepared that lost ground can be made up in a year or less.

Recommendations

A. Texas should evaluate the use of the Preliminary Scholastic Assessment Test/National Merit Scholarship Qualifying Test and/or the PLAN tests to measure achievement in English, math, reading, and science in 10th grade students.

Most colleges and universities across the United States use student scores on the SAT and ACT, with other factors, to determine eligibility for admission. Both of these tests have been around for decades and have proved to be a steady measure of potential success in higher education. PSAT and PLAN tests the precursors to the SAT and ACT are given in the 10th grade and earlier. Texas should use what the majority of universities and colleges use as a measure of achievement in the areas that are important to institution of higher education.

B. Texas should evaluate the use of the SAT and ACT tests to evaluate college readiness.

As mentioned above these tests set the standard for admission to institutions of higher education across the nation. These scores could be used to identify what areas a student needs help with and make testing the diagnostic tool it was meant to be.

C. The state should develop and fully fund a short intervention tutorial program for students in need of remedial education.

Following the lead of the University of Texas at El Paso and its area's 12 school districts, the state should require that the Texas Higher Education Coordinating Board and the Texas Education Agency develop a program that uses established assessment tools and short intervention tutorial programs to address the need for remedial education. Sometimes students need only a few hours of refresher lessons to test into college-level work. The legislature, in 2009, appropriated $5 million to get the program started while spending almost $80 million on its standardized testing program.

It's Time to Rethink How
To Fund Public Education

Summary

The Texas system of funding public education is once again being challenged in the courts. This has been an ongoing struggle for over 30 years. This time it was spurred by the 82nd Legislature's reduction in what the state provides to local districts to supplement their local tax efforts. There is no doubt that this struggle will continue as long as Texas relies on local property taxes for the bulk of its public education funding. There are a number of things the state should consider to both free up more money to be used on instruction, and to bring a sense of fairness to what is spent on each child's education.

Background

Not long after the 82nd legislative special session adjourned 6 lawsuits were filed in district court in Austin, Texas asking that the court find the system of public school finance unconstitutional because it is not efficient. The tussle over school funding has gone on since the 1970's. The latest round was spurred by a $5.4 billion dollar reduction in school funding by state policy makers.

The law suits center around three main issues: efficiency, adequacy, and meaningful discretion. Those arguing that the system is not efficient fall into three categories. One group argues that the system is inequitable, another argues that the cap on charter schools and the prohibition of using state funding for charter school facilities is inefficient, and the third argues that since the state doesn't know how much it costs to educate a student there is no way the system could be efficient. The adequacy issue centers on the argument that the state has failed to provide enough funding, didn't fund growth in enrollment, and didn't provide additional funds at a time when it raised accountability standards. Meaningful discretion centers on the argument that the state has imposed a statewide property tax because it limits the amount local districts can tax.

Effects of Recent Cuts

The effects of the loss of $500 per student funding has resulted in larger class sizes, fewer teachers, school closings, and fewer programs to help at-risk and special needs students. While it is too early to tell, it may well lead to higher dropout rates. These effects are more profound in low property wealth districts and in districts that have higher numbers of economically disadvantaged students. School districts across the state shed more than 25,000 jobs before the 2011-2012 school year.[40] The most frequently cut positions were teacher's aides and professional development staff.

Some school districts raised fees and taxes to help make up the difference, but that was not the case for districts such as Corpus Christi ISD where 70% of its students are economically disadvantaged. And in some cases schools have turned to t-shirt sales, fund raisers and advertising to make up the difference. These activities were traditionally used by booster clubs to fund extracurricular activities.

Current system

Local property tax revenue currently provides over 55% of the revenue in the system.[41] As long as public school funding is rooted in property taxes inequity will continue. In 2010-2011, according to the Texas Education Agency, the school districts in the top 15% of wealth had over $2 billion left in taxing capacity while districts in the bottom 15% of wealth had $0 left in taxing capacity. According to the Comptroller of Public Accounts in 2008-2009, the state spent $56.6 billion on public education. $20.3 billion (36%) was provided by the state, $31.7 billion (56%) was provided by local sources, and $4.5 billion (8%) came from Federal sources including American Reinvestment and Recovery Act monies.[42]

The current system of public school finance is a convoluted collection of weights and formulas that took a 50 page document to explain it.[43] Much of the formula weights, rules and regulations haven't been updated in decades.

Deficiencies

An example is the Cost of Education Index (CEI) which is used to adjust for the geographic variation in known resource costs and costs of education. But that index hasn't been adjusted since 1991. "Research indicates that the state could save billions by aligning the CEI with today's actual cost differentials."[44]

Another example is the state facilities funding system guarantee has not changed from the original $35 yield per penny per average daily attendance adopted in 1999 although the cost of construction has doubled since then.[45]

Identifying the costs of educating a student

Identifying the costs of educating a student is difficult at best because of the number of variables involved. For instance special needs students require more per student spending than others. Some spending is required by federal regulations. And there are regional differences in the costs of goods and salaries. The only way efficiency can be measured is if there is a benchmark to which it is compared but that benchmark does not exist.

Recommendations

A. Texas should create a task force to identify the cost of providing an efficient and equitable education on a per student basis.

Currently, the state spends about $11,000 per student for both instruction and facilities. But the amount spent varies widely by district. There are many factors that drive spending such as the number of disadvantaged students or the number of special needs students that reside in a district. The task force would take all such variables into account in determining a target figure. The task force should utilize the resources of our state universities, the Texas Education Agency, The Comptroller of Public Accounts, and the Department of Information Resources, among others.

B. Texas should reexamine the need for the many reports, studies and regulations it imposes on local independent school districts.

Many of the reports and regulations are mandated by the legislature in response to complaints by parents and in many cases by special interest groups. The best type of control is local control. If parents and taxpayers don't want to pay for certain information their school districts shouldn't be forced to spend the money to produce that information. And decentralizing the control of schools will allow taxpayers to decide if their schools are doing a good job of educating their children.

C. The legislature should consider utilizing a block grant funding approach when providing state monies to local districts using state monies to equalize the amount spent on educating children.

One of the major problems with the current system of school finance is its reliance on property taxes which varies widely between districts. Some districts are taxing at the maximum level allowed by law, or allowed by the local economy. Others are not.

Once a target amount of per student spending is established money provided by the state should be used to help districts achieve that number. The idea is that if a district is taxing at the limits allowed by law and collecting 95% of those taxes and can't reach the target amount state dollars would be used to make up the difference. This type of funding puts the local taxpayers in charge of their local district's spending and will allow them to decide if their districts are spending the money wisely.

D. Require publishers to provide textbooks in a format compatible with common electronic reading devices.

This recommendation by the Comptroller in her Financial Allocation Study for Texas report makes sense. Better use of technology can reduce certain costs that could then be used to fund instruction. She estimated that doing so will save $84 million dollars a year. That money could then be used to help equalize spending at the district level.

E. Texas should update the weights used to determine funding levels.

As mentioned many indices used haven't been updated since the 1990's and do not accurately reflect costs in today's economy. As long as out dated data is used Texas cannot fund education adequately.

Use Technology to Reduce
the Cost of Higher Education

Summary

The cost of higher education has risen faster than the cost of medical care in the United States and the cost of course materials has risen faster than the rate of inflation. Students are graduating with record debt in the form of student loans and pre-paid tuition programs are having a hard time making good on their promises. But not all is gloom and doom; there is a light at the end of the tunnel. And the way is being lit by technology.

Background

Texas institutions of higher education, led by the Texas Higher Education Coordinating Board (THECB), have done well in the utilization of instructional technology. There are hundreds of on line courses available to students through individual two year and four year institutions, technical colleges, and virtual networks. But more can and should be done. Like most areas, education is stuck in a costly bricks and mortar mindset. Its focus is on face to face instruction with little regard the savings that the use of technology can bring. According to the THECB, in 2011 alone, institutions were expected to pay over $17 billion in capital costs. Almost half of the capital costs are for in new construction and a third of it for repair and renovation of existing facilities. But less than 1% was expected to be spent on information resources.[46]

Not only is education stuck in the bricks and mortar mindset but it is also stuck in the printed and bound mindset. "According to Barbara Chow of the Hewlett Foundation, 'another study found that 60% of the students who dropped out of college said that the cost of textbooks and other expenses besides tuition had affected them financially."[47] This year students will spend over $1000 for books and supplies. These costs can be minimized by students who purchase used books or rent books when available. They can also recover some of the cost at the end of a semester by selling their books to resellers or other students. More can be saved by the purchase of e-texts although those come with a time limit and cannot be resold.

One avenue being explored by educators is the use of open education resources. These texts can be purchased from online retailers such as Amazon for as little as $5. They can also be purchased as printed volumes or even printed and bound volumes for far less than the $100-$200 cost of traditional text books. Other advantages to OER are that information can be tailored to a specific instructor's and/or student's needs and information can be updated immediately. Open course libraries have been developed in other states that have saved students as much as $100 per course. Rice University has developed OER through its Connexions program. The program has used private funding to develop the course material so far.

If Texas wants a highly educated and skilled workforce it must make better use of technology to reduce costs. Once again, those who attend institutions of higher education are hit with both the amount of taxes they pay, the cost of goods they buy as a consumer that are taxed, and the direct expenditures to the institutions they attend. Anything we as policy makers can do to lesson that burden should and must be done if we are to continue to attract business and experience continued economic prosperity.

Recommendations

A. Move more classes on line

While Texas has done a good job of developing online courses, much more can be done. The Higher Education Coordinating Board should continue to work with the major university and community college systems to make more courses available on line to avoid the need for the construction and maintenance of instructional facilities.

B. The state should create and fully fund the Texas Open Source Digital Library.

This recommendation offered by Dr. Sydney Burris of Rice University makes a great deal of sense and can make college affordable for thousands of Texas families. It is recommended that course materials be developed for texts that cover 80% of the courses in our educational system and that instructors are incentivized to use them.

C. Digitize libraries

Other cost savings can be achieved by digitizing libraries and doing away with the need for bricks and mortar facilities. In 2011, the state could have saved $300 million in new construction costs by eliminating the need for library facilities. This does not count the cost of maintenance and operations, and renovations of existing library facilities. Nor does it cover the cost of replacement or repair of the books themselves.

About the Author

Raul Torres served in the Texas House of Representatives from 2011 through 2013 where he represented District 33 in Corpus Christi.

Raul is a licensed Certified Public Accountant and has owned and operated Raul Torres, CPA, a full service accounting and financial services firm, since 1993. He graduated from Corpus Christi State University with a Bachelor of Business Administration with a major in Accounting and a minor in Finance. He obtained a Masters of Business Administration degree from Texas A&M University-Corpus Christi in 1994.

In addition to being a licensed CPA, he is also a President of Freedom Tax Services, Inc, a Liberty Tax Service franchisee, and owner of Raul Torres Insurance Agency. He is a member of the Texas Society of Certified Public Accountants and the International Association of Registered Financial Consultants, Inc.

While in the Texas House of Representatives, Raul served on the Appropriations and Insurance Committees. He authored key legislation, SB 563, which was designed to eliminate wasteful government spending. He also carried legislation to bring additional economic development and jobs to the city of Corpus Christi. He also carried legislation returning approximately $77 million from the state to cities and counties, resulting in his being honored with Texas Municipal League's Legislator of the Year Award for 2011. He also earned the Texas Association of Benefit Administrator's "Top Ten Legislator" Award, and the Texas Association of Business "Fighter of Free Enterprise" Award for his support of the business community.

Raul is active in community service. He previously served on the Loan Review Board and the Traffic Advisory Board for the City of Corpus Christi. Raul has been involved and has supported local youth sports programs and band booster clubs. Raul and his wife Gina are proud parents of five children and seven grandchildren and are members of the Church of Christ.

Endnotes

1   Carroll, Conn, "Study: States over $4 trillion in debt," The Washington Examiner, August 29, 2012.

2   The Texas Workforce Commission, "Rapid Process Improvement: Work Opportunity Tax Credit Program," Report to the 82nd Legislature, August 1, 2012. p. [1]

3   Friedlander, Blaine P., Jr., "Grad researchers tell state lawmakers what attracts businesses," Cornell Chronicle, Vol. 27, Number 36, June 6, 1996. Internet document http://www.news.cornell.edu/chronicle/96/6.6.96/NYbusiness.html

4   Combs, Susan, "Texas Ahead: Economic Development and Business Development Expenditures," January 2011. Web page: http://www.texasahead.org/economy/sb275/ecodevexp.php. Last viewed 9/19/2012.

5   Copelin, Laylan, "Experts: Texas creating jobs, but faces challenges," Austin American Statesman, September 5, 2012.

6   Texas Constitution, article VII, section 1 ("A general diffusion of knowledge being essential to the preservation of the liberties and rights of the people, it shall be the duty of the Legislature of the State to establish and make suitable provision for the support and maintenance of an efficient system of public free schools.")

7   Texas Comptroller of Public Accounts, "Texas Performance Review: Against the Grain: High-Quality, Low-Cost Government for Texas ED 8 Reduce the Need for Post-Secondary Remedial Education by Holding Public

Secondary Schools Accountable", January 1993. http://www.window.state.tx.us/tpr/atg/atged/atged08.html

8   Cargile, Erin, "Tests' price tag $90 million this year," KXAN report, May 4, 2012. http://www.kxan.com/dpp/news/investigations/staars-price-tag-90-million-this-year

9   Dexheimer, Eric, "The high cost of TAKS," Austin American Statesman, March 19, 2009. http://mo.statesman.com/blogs/content/shared-gen/blogs/austin/investigative/entries/2009/03/19/the_high_cost_of_taks.html

10   Simon, Stephanie, "Parents Protest Surge in Standardized Testing," Reuters, 6/12/2012. www.reutersreprints.com.

11   Smith, Morgan, "Design Flaw Suspected In Texas Standardized Tests," The Texas Tribune, July 30, 2012. http://www.texastribune.org/texas-education/public-education/design-flaw-suspected-texas-standardized-tests/print/

12   Edgewood Independent School District et all vs. Scott filed (Dist. Ct., Travis County Texas) at 26.

13   Texas Comptroller of Public Accounts, Financial Allocation Study for Texas, www.fastexas.org, accessed 8/20/2012.

14   The Texas Education Agency, "School Finance 101: Funding of Texas Public Schools," January 2011.

15   Fort Bend Independent School District et al., vs. Scott, No. D-1-GV-11-002028 (200th Dist. Ct. Travis County Texas) at 14.

16   The Texas Taxpayer & Student Fairness Coalition et al., vs. Scott, no. D-1-GN-11-003130, (200th Dist. Ct., Travis County Texas) p. 8

[17] The Texas Higher Education Coordinating Board, "Capital Expenditure Plans: FY 2011 to FY 2015," August, 2010, p. 7.

[18] Burrus, Sidney, PhD., Rice University, testimony before the Senate Higher Education Committee, 6/13/12.

[19] Anatomy of a Priority-Based Budget Process, SHAYNE C. KAVANAGH, JON JOHNSON, AND CHRIS FABIAN. Government Finance Review, Date: April 2010, Volume/issue: Vol. 26, No. 2

[20] Perry, Rick, "Perry: Budget compact gets lawmakers back to doing things 'the Texas way'," Fort Worth Star Telegram, 4/20/2012.

[21] Memorandum, From Governor's Office of Budget, Planning and Policy and the Texas Legislative Budget Board to State Agency Board/Commission Chairs, State Agency Heads/ Executive Directors, Appellate Court Justices and Judges, Chancellors, Presidents, and Directors of Institutions and Agencies of Higher Education, June 4, 2012.

[22] Texas Legislative Budget Board document, "15 Lessons Learned."

[23] Adams, Joe, "Using a Performance Based Budgeting System: Lessons from the Texas Experience," John C. Stennis, Institute of Government, Mississippi State University, http://joe.adams. tripod.com/sitebuilderfiles/chapter_nine.pdf, p. 456.

[24] Van Landingham, Gary, "Guest blog: 13 states get on board for cutting-edge cost benefit analysis," April 17, 2012, internet document: http://cbkb.org/2012/04/guest-blog-13-states-get-on-board-for-cutting-edge-cost-benefit-analysis/, accessed July 28, 2012.

[25] Echeverri-Carroll, Elsie L.; Ayala, Sofía G., "Regulation and Competitiveness of U.S. Businesses Is It Time for a Competitive Impact Statement?" The University of Texas at Austin, 2008, p.1.

[26] The Texas Workforce Commission, "Rapid Process Improvement: Work Opportunity Tax Credit Program," Report to the 82nd Legislature, August 1, 2012. p. 1

[27] ibid, p. 21.

[28] Copelin, Laylan, "Experts: Texas creating jobs, but faces challenges," Austin American Statesman, September 5, 2012.

[29] Friedlander, Blaine P., Jr., "Grad researchers tell state lawmakers what attracts businesses," Cornell Chronicle, Vol. 27, Number 36, June 6, 1996. Internet document http://www.news.cornell.edu/chronicle/96/6.6.96/NYbusiness.html

[30] Texas Constitution, article VII, section 1 ("A general diffusion of knowledge being essential to the preservation of the liberties and rights of the people, it shall be the duty of the Legislature of the State to establish and make suitable provision for the support and maintenance of an efficient system of public free schools.")

[31] Fort Bend Independent School District, et al. vs. Scott, No. D-1-GV-11-002028, (200th Dist. Ct., Travis County, Texas.).

[32] Fort Bend Independent School District, et al. vs. Scott, No. D-1-GV-11-002028, (200th Dist. Ct., Travis County, Texas.) at 11.

[33] Texas Comptroller of Public Accounts, "Texas Performance Review: Against the Grain: High-Quality, Low-Cost Government for Texas ED 8 Reduce the Need for Post-Secondary Remedial Education by Holding Public

Secondary Schools Accountable", January 1993. http://www.window.state.tx.us/tpr/atg/atged/atged08.html

[34] Texas Comptroller of Public Accounts, "Texas Performance Review: Breaking the Mold: New Ways to Govern Texas ED12 A Review of Student Testing Programs Is Needed," July 1991. http://www.window.state.tx.us/tpr/btm/btmed/ed12.html

[35] Cargile, Erin, "Tests' price tag $90 million this year," KXAN report, May 4, 2012. http://www.kxan.com/dpp/news/investigations/staars-price-tag-90-million-this-year

[36] Dexheimer, Eric, "The high cost of TAKS," Austin American Statesman, March 19, 2009. http://www.statesman.com/blogs/content/shared-gen/blogs/austin/investigative/entries/2009/03/19/the_high_cost_of_taks.html

[37] Simon, Stephanie, "Parents Protest Surge in Standardized Testing," Reuters, 6/12/2012. www.reutersreprints.com.

[38] Dexheimer, Eric, "The high cost of TAKS," Austin American Statesman, March 19, 2009. http://www.statesman.com/blogs/content/shared-gen/blogs/austin/investigative/entries/2009/03/19/the_high_cost_of_taks.html

[39] Smith, Morgan, "Design Flaw Suspected In Texas Standardized Tests," The Texas Tribune, July 30, 2012. http://www.texastribune.org/texas-education/public-education/design-flaw-suspected-texas-standardized-tests/print/

[40] Smith, Morgan, "In Hard Times, Schools Zero In on Employees," The Texas Tribune, August 11, 2012, internet document: *http://www.nytimes.com/2012/08/12/us/texas-schools-zero-in-on-employee-numbers.html?_r=1*, accessed 8/25/2012.

41 Edgewood Independent School District et all vs. Scott filed (Dist. Ct., Travis County Texas) at 26.

42 Texas Comptroller of Public Accounts, Financial Allocation Study for Texas, www.fastexas.org, accessed 8/20/2012.

43 The Texas Education Agency, "School Finance 101: Funding of Texas Public Schools," January 2011.

44 Fort Bend Independent School District et al., vs. Scott, No. D-1-GV-11-002028 (200th Dist. Ct. Travis County Texas) at 14.

45 The Texas Taxpayer & Student Fairness Coalition et al., vs. Scott, no. D-1-GN-11-003130, (200th Dist. Ct., Travis County Texas) p. 8

46 The Texas Higher Education Coordinating Board, "Capital Expenditure Plans: FY 2011 to FY 2015," August, 2010, p. 7.

47 Burrus, Sidney, PhD., Rice University, testimony before the Senate Higher Education Committee, 6/13/12.